# Table of Contents

***About 2[g] Habitats:*** ........ **2**

***Cost:*** ........ **3**

***Color Selections:*** ........ **4**

***Color Selection Deadlines:*** ........ **12**

***10 Stages of Construction:*** ........ **16**

***Sample Budget:*** ........ **19**

***2[g] Standard Feature Option Sheet:*** ........ **33**

***Invoice:*** ........ **42**

***First Team Meeting:*** ........ **43**

***Pre-Drywall Meeting:*** ........ **46**

***Homeowner Introduction Meeting:*** ........ **49**

## About 2[g] Habitats:

Immerse yourself in the finest modern luxury living in the most exclusive areas of the DFW Metroplex with 2[g] Habitats. We set new standards for living through our clean, contemporary and modern designs created exclusively for your lifestyle.

2[g] Habitats focuses on designing and building energy efficient homes ranging from contemporary to modern in design. Every detail of a home built by 2[g] Habitats is carefully constructed ensuring a final product that delivers high performance systems, environmentally friendly materials, and fully integrated home automation. 2[g] Habitats strives to deliver unique living environments with clean lines that allow for a clutter free and peaceful ambiance. Our team will provide the professional guidance you need to design the modern home of your dreams.

2[g] Habitats prides itself on master craftsmanship, attention to detail and the strict adherence to the architectural vision to ensure your new home encompasses the one of a kind feeling you call home.

Our extensive operational background has resulted in many streamlined processes creating cost savings for our customers without sacrificing quality. With over 15 years of experience in the home building industry, 2[g] Habitats is defined by our commitment to building strong vendor and customer relationships, designing original architectural floor plans and delivering unparalleled levels of customer service.

We create your home to look like a striking canvas with modern curb appeal, courtyards that open to the stars, tranquil outdoor living areas with fire pits and outdoor kitchens, dramatic windows, gourmet kitchens, spa inspired master suites and state-of-the-art entertaining areas.

## Cost:

"At 2g Habitats, we want your home construction to be as painless as possible. Why worry about constant cost overruns and time delays associated with waiting on construction bids? Wouldn't you rather enjoy peace of mind knowing exactly what you are buying at the time of contract, and be able to concentrate on life after construction?

For these reasons, and many more, we have implemented a fixed cost structure for all of our "build to suit" engagements. Rather than operate on a "cost plus" scenario that can lead to inaccurate bidding and time delays, we build our homes anywhere from $180 to $300 per square foot. *

We are very involved in every aspect of the construction process. We manage every detail so that you don't have to. For this service, we charge an 20% management fee for general contracting. This fee covers the management of all construction costs.

Building a custom home doesn't have to be a stressful process. We have 100's of homes under our belt and have developed a very collaborative, yet simple, process for exceeding your expectations. We include the highest level of standard features of any custom builder in our market, and invite you to compare our offerings with all perspective builders you may be interviewing. We look forward to serving you."

*Does not include price of lot

# Color Selections:

| Exterior Selections: | | |
|---|---|---|
| Stucco | | |
| Cast Stone | | |
| Exterior Paint | | |
| Front Door Style | | |
| Gutters | | |
| Roof Shingles | | |
| Window Frames | | |
| Master Bath Window | | |
| Garage Door | | |
| **Stair Parts:** | | |
| Baluster Style | | |
| Caps & Risers | | |
| Starter Step | | |
| Handrail | | |
| **Wood Floors:** | | |
| Wood Type | | |
| Location | | |
| **Fireplace Types:** | | |
| Family Room | Type | |
| | Size | |
| Master Bedroom | Type | |
| Exterior | Type | |

| Interior Paint Selections: | |
|---|---|
| Walls | |
| Ceilings | |
| Trim | |
| Accent | |
| Skip Trowel | |
| Rounded Corners | |
| Interior Stain | |
| **Cabinets:** | |
| Kitchen | |
| Butler's Pantry | |
| Wet Bar | |
| Utility | |
| Powder | |
| Bath 2 | |
| Bath 3 | |
| Bath 4 | |
| Master Bath | |

| Appliances: | | |
|---|---|---|
| Range | Model # | |
| | Manufacture # | |
| Vent Hood | Model # | |
| | Manufacture # | |
| Microwave | Model # | |
| | Manufacture # | |
| Dishwasher | Model # | |
| | Manufacture # | |
| Refrigerator | Model # | |
| | Manufacture # | |

| Bath Hardware: | |
|---|---|
| Powder Bath | |
| Bath 2 | |
| Bath 3 | |
| Bath 4 | |
| Master Bath | |

| Mirrors: | |
|---|---|
| Powder Bath | |
| Bath 2 | |
| Bath 3 | |
| Bath 4 | |
| Master Bath | |

<table>
<tr><th colspan="3">Plumbing:</th></tr>
<tr><td>Kitchen Sink</td><td colspan="2"></td></tr>
<tr><td>Kitchen Faucet</td><td colspan="2"></td></tr>
<tr><td>Powder Bath Sink</td><td colspan="2"></td></tr>
<tr><td>Powder Bath Faucet</td><td colspan="2"></td></tr>
<tr><td>Bath 2 Sink</td><td colspan="2"></td></tr>
<tr><td>Bath 2 Faucet</td><td colspan="2"></td></tr>
<tr><td>Bath 3 Sink</td><td colspan="2"></td></tr>
<tr><td>Bath 3 Faucet</td><td colspan="2"></td></tr>
<tr><td>Bath 4 Sink</td><td colspan="2"></td></tr>
<tr><td>Bath 5 Faucet</td><td colspan="2"></td></tr>
<tr><td>Master Sink</td><td colspan="2"></td></tr>
<tr><td>Master Faucet</td><td colspan="2"></td></tr>
<tr><td>Commodes</td><td colspan="2"></td></tr>
<tr><td rowspan="2">Master Tub</td><td>Model/Color</td><td></td></tr>
<tr><td>Manufacture</td><td></td></tr>
<tr><td>Master Shower</td><td>Glass Type</td><td></td></tr>
<tr><th colspan="3">Interior Doors & Hardware:</th></tr>
<tr><td rowspan="2">Door Style</td><td colspan="2"></td></tr>
<tr><td colspan="2"></td></tr>
<tr><td>Door Hardware</td><td colspan="2"></td></tr>
</table>

| Fireplace Surrounds: | | |
|---|---|---|
| Family Room | Style | |
| | Color | |
| Master Bedroom | Style | |
| | Color | |
| Exterior | Style | |
| **Countertops:** | | |
| Kitchen | | |
| | Edge | |
| Utility | | |
| | Edge | |
| Powder | | |
| | Edge | |
| Bath 2 | | |
| | Edge | |
| Bath 3 | | |
| | Edge | |
| Bath 4 | | |
| | Edge | |
| Master Bath | | |
| | Edge | |

| Wall Tile: | |
|---|---|
| Kitchen Backsplash | |
| Bath 2 | |
| Bath 3 | |
| Bath 4 | |
| Master Bath | |
| **Flooring:** | |
| Carpet | |
| Carpet Pad | |
| Entry | |
| Dining | |
| Study | |
| Formal Living | |
| Family Room | |
| Kitchen/Nook | |
| Butler's Pantry | |
| Utility Room | |
| Powder Bath | |
| Bath 2 | |
| Bath 3 | |
| Bath 4 | |
| Master Bath | |

<table>
<tr><th colspan="2">Miscellaneous:</th></tr>
<tr><td rowspan="3">Home Pro</td><td></td></tr>
<tr><td></td></tr>
<tr><td></td></tr>
<tr><td>Electrical Switches</td><td></td></tr>
</table>

# Color Selection Deadlines:

| Completed: | Color Selection: | Deadline: |
|---|---|---|
| **Date:** | **Critical Decision #1** | **Stage 1** |
| | Floor Plug locations determined | |
| | Foundation Venting determined | |
| | Brick/Stone/Stucco Locations Decided | |
| | Floor levels/selections defined (wood, tile, carpet) | |
| | Gas stub out locations decided | |
| | House bib locations decided | |
| | Window decisions complete | |
| | Roofing materials selected | |
| | Exterior door selections complete | |
| | First team meeting checklist complete | |
| | | |
| | **Critical Decision #2** | **Stage 1** |
| | Appliances selected | |
| | Plumbing fixtures selected | |
| | Bath hardware selected | |
| | Bathtubs selected | |
| | Garage door/Pulldowns selected | |
| | Fireplaces Selected | |
| | | |

| | **Critical Decision #3** | **Stage 2** |
|---|---|---|
| | Countertops selected | |
| | Flooring selected | |
| | Electric light fixtures selected | |
| | Gas lamp fixtures selected | |
| | Outdoor kitchen items selected | |
| | Type of dryer determined (Gas/Electric) | |
| | Limestone/Cast Stone selections complete (Fireplace/Vent hood) | |
| | | |
| | **Critical Decision #4** | **Stage 3** |
| | High Voltage decisions complete | |
| | Low Voltage decisions complete | |
| | Cabinet Selections complete | |
| | Trim selections complete | |
| | Interior door selections complete | |
| | Stair parts selected | |
| | | |

| | Critical Decision #5 | Stage 4 |
|---|---|---|
| | Stone samples selected | |
| | Brick samples selected | |
| | Stucco samples selected | |
| | Exterior paint samples selected | |
| | Interior pain samples selected | |
| | Stain samples selected | |
| | | |
| | Critical Decision #6 | Stage 5 |
| | Landscape Design selected | |
| | Fence selected | |
| | Flatwork locations chosen | |
| | Door hardware selected | |
| | Cabinet Hardware selected | |
| | Bath hardware selected | |
| | | |

# 10 Stages of Construction:

Building your new home is a detailed, multi-step process. 2[g] Habitats' 10 Stages of Construction will help you track your home's progress with a better understanding of the major activities that take place during each phase.

| Stage 1 - Preconstruction |
|---|
| During the preconstruction phase is when all the behind the scenes work is being performed including: Architectural Plans, Plot Plans, Budgeting, Design Selections, Contracts, Team Meetings, and Permits. While at times it may seem like nothing is happening at this stage, this is one of the most important stages of construction as it details how your new home will come together. |
| **Stage 2 - Foundation** |
| This is when the lot is prepared and graded, forms are set, all plumbing grounds are completed, and the concrete is poured. Your foundation is the single most important aspect of your home. During this stage city and engineer inspections will be completed to ensure your foundations integrity. |
| **Stage 3 - Frame** |
| Now your home will begin to take shape. One day there will just be a slab and the next you will have the beginnings of a home! During the frame stage all of your walls, joists, rafters, beams and roof will be completed providing what will be the skeleton for your new home. This is when you will begin to get a feel for your new home's layout. |
| **Stage 4 - Mechanicals** |
| Your major mechanical systems are installed once your home is dried in. These include electrical, HVAC, and plumbing systems. This is a key time as the majority of your design selections will need to be completed to keep construction on schedule. This is also a critical point in time as numerous inspections will be performed – both municipal and 3rd party. |
| **Stage 5 – Sheetrock/Exterior Finishes** |
| Once all the major mechanicals have been inspected, your home will be insulated, and the interior and exterior surfaces of your home will be applied. Sheetrock and texture will be completed on the interior of your home. On the exterior siding, stucco, brick and/or stone will be applied per your design specifications. |

Before you know it, you will be halfway through the homebuilding process. Learn more about stages 6 through 10.

| Stage 6 – Trim, Doors and Cabinets |
|---|
| The trim, interior doors and cabinets (if painted) will be installed at this time. The trim includes crown mold, baseboards, chair rail, and any door casings. If you are getting nail-down wood floors they will also be installed at this time along with your stairs, risers and balusters if they are wood. There will be some areas where it might look like trim is missing. The trim in these areas will be installed once the tile and stone details are completed in those locations. This is when your house starts to feel more like a home. |

| Stage 7 – Paint and Countertops |
|---|
| Your home will be primed, prepped and painted. Once the paint has cured, your countertops and natural stone (limestone, cast stone or concrete) details will be installed at the locations you have chosen such as at fireplaces or range hoods or accent walls. |

| Stage 8 – Fixtures and Flooring |
|---|
| The finishing touches go in now – plumbing fixtures, electrical trim, HVAC controllers and condensers, door hardware, cabinet hardware, mirrors, and shower glass. All of your tile, carpet and engineered flooring will go in at this time. This is where all of your color selections that have been made over the last several months come together and make your home look stunning. |

| Stage 9 – Builder Acceptance |
|---|
| Builder acceptance only occurs after not only 2[g] Habitats' staff, but also our 3rd party inspectors, municipal inspectors and energy inspectors have performed a thorough inspection of your home to ensure it meets 2[g] Habitats' standards of excellence. |

| Stage 10 – Homeowner Introduction |
|---|
| This is when you are introduced to your new home. We will go over all the systems in your home (appliances, plumbing, electrical, and HVAC), care and maintenance items, sprinkler operation, and more. This is your time to ask questions and learn about your home inside and out. Congratulations on your new home! |

# Sample Budget:

123 Wallabee Way
New Construction
Draft 1
December 2, 2020

| Cost Code | Category | Budget | Notes |
|---|---|---|---|
| 100 | LOT COST & LAND DEVELOPMENT | | |
| 101 | Lot Purchase | | |
| 112 | Real Estate Commission | | |
| 113 | Legal Fees-Lot Purchase | | |
| 114 | Appraisals-Lot Purchase | | |
| 115 | Lot Closing Costs | | |
| 116 | Interest on Lot | | |
| 120 | Real Estate Taxes | | |
| 1000 | PERMITS & FEES | | |
| 1010 | Building Permits | | |
| 1011 | Permits - Tap Fees | | |
| 1030 | Watershed Permit | | |
| 1040 | DNR Permit | | |
| 1090 | Misc Permits and Fees | | |
| 1100 | ARCHITECTURAL & ENGINEERING | | |
| 1105 | Architectural / Design Fees | | |
| 1106 | Interior Designer Fee | | |
| 1114 | Plot Plan Fee | | |
| 1115 | Blueprints & Copies | | |
| 1118 | Survey Lot Stake | | |
| 1119 | Form Survey | | |
| 1120 | Surveys | | |
| 1121 | Soils Testing | | |
| 1123 | Geotechnical Engineering | | |
| 1124 | Engineering - Frame | | |
| 1125 | Engineering - Foundation | | |

| | | | |
|---|---|---|---|
| 1126 | Engineering - Structural Steel | | |
| 1127 | Engineering - Other | | |
| 1128 | Foundation Inspection | | |
| 1129 | Independent Final Inspect | | |
| 1130 | Construction Documentation | | |
| 1200 | SITE WORK | | |
| 1220 | Tree Clearing | | |
| 1221 | Stump Grinding | | |
| 1223 | Root Barrier | | |
| 1225 | Erosion Control | | |
| 1245 | Street Cleaning & Sweeping | | |
| 1250 | Retaining Wall | | |
| 1251 | Retaining Wall - Engineered | | |
| 1299 | Site Work-Extras | | |
| 1300 | DEMOLITION | | |
| 1310 | Demolition | | |
| 1311 | Demo - Stone Elevation | | |
| 1312 | Demo - Sheetrock | | |
| 1313 | Demo - Frame | | |
| 1314 | Demo - Concrete Fence | | |
| 1319 | Demolition Extras | | |
| 1320 | Utility Disconnects | | |
| 1330 | Well Abandonment | | |
| 1340 | Lead Remediation | | |
| 1400 | UTILITY CONNECTIONS | | |
| 1405 | Well | | |
| 1406 | Septic System | | |
| 1410 | Water Connection | | |
| 1420 | Sewer Connection | | |
| 1430 | Sewer & Water Connection | | |
| 1460 | Gas Service | | |
| 1470 | Electric Service | | |
| 1471 | Temporary Electric Service | | |
| 1472 | Monthly Utility Bills During Construction | | |
| 1473 | Underground Electric Service | | |
| 1480 | Telephone Service | | |
| 1490 | Other Utility Connects | | |
| 1500 | CONSTRUCTION PERIOD FINANCING | | |

| | | | |
|---|---|---|---|
| 1503 | Loan Origination Fee | | |
| 1505 | Loan Discount | | |
| 1510 | Construction Interest | | |
| 1530 | Appraisals for Financing | | |
| 1535 | Financing Fees/Wire Fees | | |
| 2000 | EXCAVATION | | |
| 2006 | Clear and Grub | | |
| 2009 | Grade - Lot Bench | | |
| 2010 | Excavation & Backfill | | |
| 2011 | Grade - Rough | | |
| 2012 | Grade - Final | | |
| 2013 | Trenching | | |
| 2014 | Grade - Final Fill Material | | |
| 2015 | Excavation Materials | | |
| 2020 | Soil Correction | | |
| 2029 | Excavation & Backfill - Extras | | |
| 2100 | FOUNDATION & CONCRETE | | |
| 2103 | Foundation - Labor | | |
| 2104 | Foundation - Pump | | |
| 2105 | Foundation - Turnkey | | |
| 2106 | Flatwork - Culvert for Drainage | | |
| 2107 | Flatwork - Interior | | |
| 2108 | Flatwork - Interior & Exterior | | |
| 2109 | Flatwork - Exterior | | |
| 2110 | Front Stoop | | |
| 2111 | Flatwork - Texture/Finish | | |
| 2120 | Pilings, Geo-Piers, Grade Beam | | |
| 2122 | Soil Conditioning - Chemical | | |
| 2123 | Soil Conditioning - Moisture | | |
| 2130 | Footings/Foundation-Extras | | |
| 2150 | CONCRETE - OTHER | | |
| 2151 | Lightweight Concrete | | |
| 2160 | Precast Plank (Span Crete) | | |
| 2165 | Rigid Foam Under Concrete | | |
| 2170 | Concrete - Extras | | |
| 2200 | WATERPROOFING | | |
| 2205 | Waterproofing | | |
| 2210 | Foundation Insulation | | |

| | | | |
|---|---|---|---|
| 2220 | Waterproof Garage Floor | | |
| 2230 | Other Waterproofing | | |
| 2240 | Caulking / Sealants | | |
| 3000 | STRUCTURAL STEEL | | |
| 3010 | Steel Fabrication & Materials | | |
| 3020 | Steel Installation | | |
| 3099 | Structural Steel-Extras | | |
| 3100 | FRAMING MATERIALS | | |
| 3110 | Framing Lumber | | |
| 3112 | Decking / Porch Materials | | |
| 3114 | Siding, Soffit & Fascia Matls | | |
| 3115 | Soffit & Fascia Materials | | |
| 3116 | Siding | | |
| 3120 | Framing Materials-Extras | | |
| 3130 | Exterior Trim, Shutters, Etc... | | |
| 3131 | Specialty Details, Columns | | |
| 3132 | Reclaimed Siding Material | | |
| 3134 | Floor Joists - engineered | | |
| 3135 | Trusses - Roof & Floor | | |
| 3136 | Steel | | |
| 3150 | FRAMING LABOR | | |
| 3151 | Frame Labor - Walls | | |
| 3152 | Frame Labor - Rafters | | |
| 3153 | Frame Labor - Cornice & Decking | | |
| 3154 | Frame Labor - Retainage | | |
| 3155 | Framing Labor | | |
| 3156 | Frame Labor - New Window/Door Openings | | |
| 3157 | Frame Labor - Existing Space Reframe | | |
| 3159 | Siding Material & Labor | | |
| 3160 | Siding Labor | | |
| 3161 | Shingle Siding Material/Labor | | |
| 3162 | Attic Access Ladder | | |
| 3165 | Soffit & Fascia Labor | | |
| 3167 | Reclaimed Siding Labor | | |
| 3170 | Exterior Trim Details | | |
| 3175 | Deck / Porch Labor | | |
| 3180 | Window Installation | | |
| 3190 | Framing Labor - Extras | | |

| | | | |
|---|---|---|---|
| 3500 | SHEET METAL | | |
| 3510 | Gutters and Downspouts | | |
| 3530 | Soffits/Gables | | |
| 3540 | Metal Flashings | | |
| 3541 | Reclaimed Tin Siding Material | | |
| 3542 | Reclaimed Tin Siding Labor | | |
| 3543 | Metal Siding | | |
| 3590 | Sheet Metal - Extras | | |
| 3600 | PLUMBING | | |
| 3610 | Plumbing | | |
| 3611 | Plumbing - Rough | | |
| 3612 | Plumbing - Top Out | | |
| 3613 | Plumbing - Trim | | |
| 3614 | Gas Lines | | |
| 3615 | Water Heaters | | |
| 3616 | Bathtubs | | |
| 3619 | Plumbing Fixtures - Install Labor | | |
| 3620 | Plumbing Fixtures | | |
| 3621 | Plumbing Fixtures - Gas Lamps | | |
| 3635 | Softener / Filters / R.O. | | |
| 3655 | Water Purification (R.O.) | | |
| 3660 | R.O. Faucet Allowance | | |
| 3685 | Plumbing Repairs | | |
| 3690 | Plumbing Extras | | |
| 3691 | Propane Tank | | |
| 3692 | Fire Sprinklers | | |
| 3700 | ELECTRICAL | | |
| 3710 | Electrical Wiring | | |
| 3711 | Electric - Rough | | |
| 3712 | Electric - Trim | | |
| 3720 | Electrical Fixtures | | |
| 3721 | Can Lights | | |
| 3790 | Electrical Extras | | |
| 3791 | Solar Panels | | |
| 3800 | HEATING & COOLING | | |
| 3801 | HVAC - Rough | | |
| 3802 | HVAC - Trim | | |
| 3803 | HVAC - Upgrades | | |

| | | | |
|---|---|---|---|
| 3810 | Heating & Cooling | | |
| 3820 | Radiant In-Floor Heat | | |
| 3830 | Insulation for In-Floor Heat | | |
| 3840 | Make-Up Air | | |
| 3890 | Heating & Cooling - Extras | | |
| 3900 | LOW VOLTAGE, AUDIO, VIDEO, CENTRAL VAC | | |
| 3910 | Low Voltage Package | | |
| 3911 | Security System | | |
| 3920 | Audio / Video System | | |
| 3930 | Intercom | | |
| 3935 | Phone / TV Pre-Wire | | |
| 3940 | Stereo Prewire | | |
| 3950 | Central Vac | | |
| 3980 | Network Pre-Wire | | |
| 3990 | Low Voltage/Security/AV/Central Vac-Extras | | |
| 4000 | ROOFING | | |
| 4010 | Roofing Materials & Labor | | |
| 4020 | Flat Roofing | | |
| 4030 | Roofing - Metal | | |
| 4080 | Flat Roof Pavers | | |
| 4089 | Roofing - Architectural Details | | |
| 4090 | Roofing - Extras | | |
| 4100 | MASONRY | | |
| 4101 | Stone Labor | | |
| 4102 | Stone Material | | |
| 4110 | Exterior Brick & Stone | | |
| 4111 | Exterior Brick | | |
| 4112 | Exterior Stone | | |
| 4113 | Lintels | | |
| 4115 | Interior Brick & Stone | | |
| 4116 | Masonry Labor | | |
| 4117 | Fireplace Surrounds | | |
| 4118 | Hearth & Mantle Stone | | |
| 4119 | Special Mortar Finish | | |
| 4120 | Special Brick Details | | |
| 4130 | Flagstone / Paving Stone Floor | | |
| 4180 | Glass Block | | |

| | | | |
|---|---|---|---|
| 4190 | Masonry-Extras | | |
| 4200 | FIREPLACE | | |
| 4210 | Fireplace - Gas | | |
| 4211 | Fireplace -Options | | |
| 4212 | Fireplace - Isokern | | |
| 4215 | Fireplace - Wood Burning | | |
| 4220 | Fireplace - Masonry | | |
| 4250 | Fireplace - Chimney Cap | | |
| 4290 | Fireplace - Extras | | |
| 4500 | WINDOWS & DOORS | | |
| 4510 | Windows - Material | | |
| 4511 | Windows - Install Labor | | |
| 4520 | Skylights | | |
| 4530 | Storm & Screen Doors | | |
| 4535 | Front Door | | |
| 4536 | Wrought Iron Entry Gate | | |
| 4537 | Front Doors - Additional | | |
| 4540 | Exterior Doors | | |
| 4541 | Interior Doors | | |
| 4542 | Thresholds and Weather Stripping | | |
| 4570 | Garage Doors | | |
| 4571 | Garage Door Openers | | |
| 4590 | Window & Door Extras | | |
| 4700 | INSULATION | | |
| 4720 | Insulation | | |
| 4721 | Foam Insulation - Walls | | |
| 4722 | Foam Insulation - Attic | | |
| 4750 | Home Seal Foam | | |
| 4760 | Sound Abatement | | |
| 4780 | Blower Door Testing | | |
| 4789 | Tyvek House Wrap | | |
| 4790 | Insulation - Extras | | |
| 4900 | PAINTING | | |
| 4910 | Paint - Exterior | | |
| 4915 | Paint - Interior | | |
| 4919 | Paint - Touchup | | |
| 4930 | Paint - Garage | | |
| 4931 | Paint - Fence Stain | | |

| | | | |
|---|---|---|---|
| 4932 | Paint - Interior Stain | | |
| 4940 | Paint - Epoxy Floors | | |
| 4985 | Paint - Faux Finishing | | |
| 4986 | Paint - Cabinets | | |
| 4987 | Paint - Windows | | |
| 4989 | Paint - Final | | |
| 4990 | Paint - Extras | | |
| 5000 | DRYWALL | | |
| 5010 | Drywall Materials & Labor | | |
| 5012 | Quiet Rock | | |
| 5013 | Resilient Channel | | |
| 5014 | Acoustic Blanket | | |
| 5020 | Drywall Texturing | | |
| 5022 | Hand Texture | | |
| 5048 | Acoustical Ceiling | | |
| 5049 | Drywall - Extras | | |
| 5050 | STUCCO | | |
| 5055 | Stucco - Material & Labor | | |
| 5056 | Stucco - Lathe and Prep | | |
| 5057 | Stucco - Material | | |
| 5058 | Stucco - Labor | | |
| 5059 | Stucco - Sand and Lintels | | |
| 5060 | Stucco - Extras | | |
| 5100 | FLOORING | | |
| 5110 | Carpet -Turnkey | | |
| 5115 | Rubber Floor | | |
| 5120 | Vinyl Floor - Turnkey | | |
| 5125 | Concrete Flooring | | |
| 5129 | Hardwood - Low VOC Stain & Poly | | |
| 5130 | Hardwood Flooring | | |
| 5131 | Engineered Flooring | | |
| 5132 | Flooring Protection | | |
| 5133 | Stairs and Risers | | |
| 5134 | Shoe Mold | | |
| 5149 | Flooring -Other | | |
| 5150 | MILLWORK | | |
| 5151 | Millwork Package | | |
| 5152 | Cedar Details - Exterior | | |

| | | | |
|---|---|---|---|
| 5153 | Cedar Details - Interior | | |
| 5155 | Interior Ironwork | | |
| 5159 | Millwork Extras | | |
| 5200 | FINISH CARPENTRY | | |
| 5230 | Trim Carpentry | | |
| 5231 | Trim Carpentry - 2nd | | |
| 5250 | Trim Carpentry - Extras | | |
| 5251 | Stairs - Front | | |
| 5252 | Stairs - Rear | | |
| 5253 | California Closets | | |
| 5270 | HARDW ARE | | |
| 5271 | Interior Door Hardware | | |
| 5272 | Exterior Door Hardware | | |
| 5273 | Interior / Exterior Door Hardware | | |
| 5274 | Cabinet Hardware | | |
| 5275 | Address Plaque, Mailbox | | |
| 5290 | Trim Carpentry - Extras | | |
| 5295 | Sauna - Materials & Labor | | |
| 5300 | COUNTERTOPS | | |
| 5310 | Granite Tops | | |
| 5311 | Quartz Countertops | | |
| 5312 | Laminate Tops | | |
| 5313 | Solid Surface Countertops | | |
| 5314 | Butcher Block Tops | | |
| 5315 | Cultured Marble Tops | | |
| 5316 | Specialty Tops | | |
| 5320 | Counter Tops - Other | | |
| 5330 | Bar Tops | | |
| 5335 | Wood Tops | | |
| 5350 | TILE, SLATE, STONE | | |
| 5351 | Tile - Floors | | |
| 5352 | Tile - Walls | | |
| 5353 | Concrete Underlayment | | |
| 5354 | Stone Flooring | | |
| 5355 | Cast Stone Fireplace Surround | | |
| 5356 | Cast Stone Hood | | |
| 5357 | Cast Stone - Columns | | |
| 5358 | Cast Stone - Window Sills | | |

| | | | |
|---|---|---|---|
| 5359 | Cast Stone - Lintels | | |
| 5360 | Cast Stone Other | | |
| 5361 | Cast Stone - Window & Door Surrounds | | |
| 5362 | Tile and Stone Sealer | | |
| 5363 | Cast Stone - Labor | | |
| 5364 | Tile Extras | | |
| 5365 | Tile - Kitchen Backsplash | | |
| 5400 | CABINETS & CLOSETS | | |
| 5490 | Cabinets | | |
| 5495 | Closet Shelving | | |
| 5496 | Master Closet System | | |
| 5499 | Cabinets - Extras | | |
| 5500 | APPLIANCES | | |
| 5505 | Appliance Package | | |
| 5510 | Range | | |
| 5520 | Range Hood | | |
| 5525 | Oven | | |
| 5527 | Warming Tray | | |
| 5530 | Disposal | | |
| 5540 | Dishwasher | | |
| 5550 | Refrigerator | | |
| 5551 | Freezer | | |
| 5555 | Trash Compactor | | |
| 5556 | Ice Maker | | |
| 5557 | Undercounter Refrigerator | | |
| 5558 | Appliances - Outdoor | | |
| 5560 | Washer / Dryer | | |
| 5570 | Microwave | | |
| 5571 | Wet Bar Appliances | | |
| 5575 | Trim Kit | | |
| 5589 | Appliance Installation | | |
| 5590 | Appliances - Extra | | |
| 5591 | Appliance Tax | | |
| 5900 | INTERIOR DECORATION | | |
| 5905 | Interior Design Fee | | |
| 5920 | W wallpaper | | |
| 5925 | Plaster Walls and Ceilings | | |
| 5930 | Shower Doors | | |

| | | | |
|---|---|---|---|
| 5935 | Shower Doors - Frameless | | |
| 5940 | Towel & Paper Holders | | |
| 5950 | Mirrors | | |
| 5960 | Stained & Leaded Glass | | |
| 5965 | Cabinet Glass | | |
| 5966 | Glass - Shelves | | |
| 5970 | Glass - Other | | |
| 5990 | Interior Decoration - Other | | |
| 6000 | GENERAL CONDITIONS | | |
| 6001 | Cleans | | |
| 6002 | Final Interior Clean (Window's) | | |
| 6003 | Final Interior Clean II (Tub's) | | |
| 6004 | Final Interior Clean (Floors) | | |
| 6005 | Final Exterior Clean | | |
| 6006 | Re-cleans | | |
| 6009 | Temporary Fencing | | |
| 6010 | Temp. Toilet | | |
| 6011 | Dumpster | | |
| 6012 | Final Cleaning | | |
| 6013 | Ductwork Cleaning | | |
| 6014 | Weekly Sweeps | | |
| 6015 | Misc Expenses | | |
| 6016 | Equipment Rental | | |
| 6017 | Wash Flatwork | | |
| 6020 | Seasonal Conditions | | |
| 6049 | General Labor | | |
| 6050 | Project Management / Supervision | | |
| 6100 | LANDSCAPING & IRRIGATION | | |
| 6105 | Sod | | |
| 6106 | Plants | | |
| 6108 | Root Barrier | | |
| 6110 | Landscaping | | |
| 6111 | Water Collection Barrels | | |
| 6120 | Pavers | | |
| 6140 | Retaining walls - non Engineered | | |
| 6150 | Dock | | |
| 6178 | Deep Drainage Ditch | | |
| 6179 | Surface Drainage | | |

| | | | |
|---|---|---|---|
| 6180 | Irrigation - Sprinklers | | |
| 6189 | Landscape Lighting | | |
| 6190 | Landscaping/Irrigation-Extras | | |
| 6200 | DRIVEWAY | | |
| 6210 | Driveway | | |
| 6211 | Driveway - Remove Existing | | |
| 6220 | Driveway - Concrete | | |
| 6230 | Driveway - Asphalt | | |
| 6240 | Driveway - Other | | |
| 6241 | Driveway - Construction Entrance | | |
| 6300 | EXTERIOR STRUCTURES | | |
| 6331 | Fence | | |
| 6332 | Gates | | |
| 6333 | Fence - Upgrades | | |
| 6334 | Exterior Juliet Balcony | | |
| 6335 | Cedar Details | | |
| 6336 | Deck Flooring Materials | | |
| 6337 | Deck Handrail and Posts | | |
| 6340 | Splash Blocks / AC Pads | | |
| 6350 | Ornamental Iron Work | | |
| 6360 | Cupola | | |
| 6365 | Tennis Court | | |
| 6370 | Swimming Pool | | |
| 6375 | Detached Garage | | |
| 6376 | Car Lift | | |
| 6377 | Garage/Storage Shelving | | |
| 6380 | Hot Tub | | |
| 6381 | Outdoor Kitchen | | |
| 6382 | Rear Elevation Details | | |
| 6383 | Front Elevation Details | | |
| 6384 | Right Side Elevation Details | | |
| 6385 | Covered Patio | | |
| 7700 | CLOSING COST | | |
| 7710 | Title Policy | | |
| 7720 | Bank Fees | | |
| 7730 | Doc Prep/Other | | |
| 7740 | Govt/Recording Fees | | |
| 8500 | CONTINGENCIES | | |

| | | | |
|---|---|---|---|
| 8520 | Contingencies | | |
| 9000 | SALARIES AND WAGES | | |
| 9010 | Project Management / Supervision | | |
| 9020 | Laborers | | |
| 9030 | Estimators, Drafters, And Other | | |
| 9090 | Other | | |
| 9600 | UNSOLD HOME MAINTENANCE EXPENCES | | |
| 9650 | Utilities-Unsold Homes | | |
| 9660 | Maintenance-Unsold Homes | | |
| 9670 | Security-Unsold Homes | | |
| 9700 | OTHER EXPENSES | | |
| 9710 | Elevator | | |
| 9711 | Misc. Costs - See Memo | | |
| 9712 | Sauna - Materials & Labor | | |
| 9715 | Wine Cellar | | |
| 9716 | Termite Treatment | | |
| 9717 | Bathroom Remodel | | |
| 9800 | MARKETING COST | | |
| 9810 | Model Home Costs | | |
| 9820 | Sales Commissions | | |
| 9830 | Sales Office Costs | | |
| 9840 | Signage | | |
| 9990 | INSURANCE & OTHER INDIRECT COST | | |
| 9991 | Project Insurance | | |
| 9992 | Liability Insurance | | |
| 9993 | 2-10 Warranty | | |
| 9995 | Warranty | | |
| 9996 | Builder's Risk Insurance | | |
| 10000 | CONSTRUCTION FEES | | |
| 10100 | Construction Management Fee | | |
| 10101 | Owner's Representation Fee | | |
| 10102 | General Contracting Fee - 20% | | |
| TOTAL | | | |

# 2[g] Standard Feature Option Sheet:

| ID | Cost Code | Item | Detail | In Bid | Details |
|---|---|---|---|---|---|
| 1 | 1100 | **Inspections** | | | |
| 2 | | | Foundation | | |
| 3 | | | Burgess | | |
| 4 | | | Standard Green Inspection - Per Most Cities and City of Dallas | | |
| 5 | | | Advanced Green Inspection - Duct Blaster and Blower Door | | |
| 6 | | | | | |
| 7 | 6100 | **Retaining Walls** | | | |
| 8 | | | When Applicable | | |
| 9 | | | | | |
| 10 | 2100 | **Foundations** | | | |
| 11 | | | 3000 PSI Slab on Ground - Rebar | | |
| 12 | | | Post Tension Slab on Grade | | |
| 13 | | | Concrete Piers | | |
| 14 | | | Heilical Piers | | |
| 15 | | | Suspended Slab | | |
| 16 | | | | | |
| 17 | 2100 | **Pump Truck** | | | |
| 18 | | | As Required | | |
| 19 | | | | | |
| 20 | 5500 | **Underslab Venting** | | | |
| 21 | | | As required - downdraft cooktop | | |
| 22 | | | | | |
| 23 | 9716 | **Termite Pre-Treatment** | | | |
| 24 | | | Termite Pre-treatment | | |
| 25 | | | | | |
| 26 | 2100 | **Flatwork** | | | |
| 27 | | | 2500 PSI | | |
| 28 | | | Wire Mesh | | |
| 29 | | | Rebar | | |
| 30 | | | Flatwork Dowels - 18" #3 @ 24" OC | | |
| 31 | | | Redwood Expansion | | |
| 32 | | | Broom Finish | | |
| 33 | | | Exposed Aggregate | | |
| 34 | | | | | |
| 35 | 2100 | **Patio** | | | |
| 36 | | | Broom Finish | | |
| 37 | | | Exposed Aggregate | | |
| 38 | | | Tile/Stone - See Stone and Tile section | | |
| 39 | | | | | |
| 40 | 3100 | **Frame** | | | |
| 41 | | | Sub Floor - 3/4" T&G OSB | | |
| 42 | | | Sub Floor - 1 1/8" Advan Tech T&G | | |
| 43 | | | Finger Joint Studs | | |
| 44 | | | Advanced Frame | | |
| 45 | | | 2x6 Exterior Walls | | |
| 46 | | | Floor Joists - I Joists | | |
| 47 | | | Additional Attic Storage | | |
| 48 | | | | | |
| 49 | 3100 | **Cornice - Sheathing - Windbrace** | | | |
| 50 | | | 1x6 Fiber Cement - Hardie | | |
| 51 | | | Cedar (Stain Grade) | | |
| 52 | | Fascia | 2x4 | | |
| 53 | | | Metal Drip Edge | | |
| 54 | | Gables | 5/4x2 Real Trim | | |
| 55 | | | Continuous Vented Hardi Soffit at horizontal eaves (not applicable with foam) | | |
| 56 | | | Smooth or Textured (Paint Grade) | | |
| 57 | | Soffit | Smooth or Textured (Stain Grade) | | |
| 58 | | Windbrace | Dow SIS Board, Zip Board, or let-ins | | |
| 59 | | | 7/16" OSB | | |
| 60 | | | 7/16" ZIP Board 4x8 Taped | | |
| 61 | | Exterior Sheathing | Insulated Zip Board - R Rating TBD | | |
| 62 | | | 1x2 Screen | | |
| 63 | | | 4x8 Hardie Paneling | | |
| 64 | | | 1x4 T&G Aqua Seal (Paint Grade) | | |
| 65 | | Cornice Porch | 1x4 T&G Cedar (Stain Grade) | | |
| 66 | | Siding | Hardi Horizontal Siding | | |
| 67 | | | Hardi Artisan Series | | |
| 68 | | | LP Siding | | |
| 69 | | | | | |
| 70 | 4500 | Garages | | | |
| 71 | | | 2x Smooth Yellow Pine | | |
| 72 | | Garage Jambs | 2x Rough Cedar | | |
| 73 | | | Siding on 4 sides | | |
| 74 | | | Brick 4 sides | | |
| 75 | | | Brick 3 sides (siding on back) | | |
| 76 | | Detached Garage | Brick front (siding on 3 sides) | | |
| 77 | | | | | |
| 78 | 2100 | **Roof Deck** | | | |
| 79 | | | 7/16" Tech Shield OSB - non foam applications | | |
| 80 | | | 7/16" OSB - No TechShield - Foam Applications | | |

| | | | | | |
|---|---|---|---|---|---|
| 81 | | | Zip Board Roof Decking | | |
| 82 | | | Upgrade to 5/8" | | |
| 83 | | | | | |
| 84 | 4500 | **Windows** | | | |
| 85 | | | Low-E dual pane vinyl - White and Tan - Plygem, Silverline | | |
| 86 | | | Low-E dual pane Wood Windows - Andersen, Pella | | |
| 87 | | | Low-E dual pane Aluminum Clad Windows - Andersen, Marvin, Pella | | |
| 88 | | | Aluminum Windows - Heritage, Western, Jeld-wen, La Cantina | | |
| 89 | | | | | |
| 90 | | | | | |
| 91 | 4500 | **Exterior Doors** | | | |
| 92 | | | Double Bore | | |
| 93 | | | Teatrical Locks (3 point locks) | | |
| 94 | | | Metal Door | | |
| 95 | | | Fiberglass Door | | |
| 96 | | | Wood Door | | |
| 97 | | | 1/2 light | | |
| 98 | | | Full light | | |
| 99 | | | | | |
| 100 | 4500 | **Front Door** | | | |
| 101 | | | Tier 1 - 6'8" Fiberglass, 6 panel, no glass | | |
| 102 | | | Tier 2 - 6'8" Fiberglass, 6 panel, Glass | | |
| 103 | | | Tier 3 - 8'0" Wood Door, 2 panel, no glass | | |
| 104 | | | Tier 4 - 8'0" Wood Door, 2 panel, Glass | | |
| 105 | | | Tier 5 - Single Metal Entry Door | | |
| 106 | | | Tier 6 - Double Metal Entry Door | | |
| 107 | | | Tier 7 - Plan Specific | | |
| 108 | | | | | |
| 109 | 3100/5350 | **Columns** | | | |
| 110 | | | Square Hardi Columns | | |
| 111 | | | Round Columns (Metal Post) Phenolic | | |
| 112 | | | Stone Columns - Wood Post | | |
| 113 | | | Wood Columns - Square - Metal post or solid? | | |
| 114 | | | Cast Stone Columns - Metal Post - Vertical Joints | | |
| 115 | | | | | |
| 116 | 4100/5350 | **Louvers/Stucco & Brick Detail** | | | |
| 117 | | | Plastic (Phenolic) | | |
| 118 | | | Wood | | |
| 119 | | | Brock pattern | | |
| 120 | | | Cast stone Embellishment | | |
| 121 | | | | | |
| 122 | 4000 | **Roofing** | | | |
| 123 | | | 90 # Felt in Valley - 15 # Felt on Roof | | |
| 124 | | | Ice and Water Sheild on Roof | | |
| 125 | | | 3 TAB Architectural ELK 30 Year | | |
| 126 | | | 3 TAB Architectural ELK 50 Year | | |
| 127 | | | Metal Roof | | |
| 128 | | | Tile Roof | | |
| 129 | | | Slate Roof | | |
| 130 | | | Air Hawks | | |
| 131 | | | Continuous Ridge Vent | | |
| 132 | | | Radiant Barrier Decking - (No radiant barrier with foam on rafters) | | |
| 133 | | | | | |
| 134 | 3600 | **Plumbing Base** | | | |
| 135 | | | Trunck and Branch System | | |
| 136 | | | Water shut-off in garage | | |
| 137 | | | Looped System | | |
| 138 | | | Water Heater in Attic (when plan accomodates) | | |
| 139 | | | 50 gallon water heater | | |
| 140 | | | up to 2.5 baths - (1) 50 gallon water heater | | |
| 141 | | | 3 Full baths and up - (2) 50 gallon heaters | | |
| 142 | | | Recirculating Pump (Requires Tanked heater) | | |
| 143 | | | Eternal Hybrid - Tankless Technology with 15 gallon tank (can recirculate) | | |
| 144 | | | Tankless water heater x1 | | |
| 145 | | Water Heater | Tankless water heater x2 | | |
| 146 | | | Number of Hose Bibs | | |
| 147 | | | Standard Hose Bib | | |
| 148 | | Hose Bibs | Aquor Water Hydrant | | |
| 149 | | | Number of Gas Drops | | |
| 150 | | Gas Drops | | | |
| 151 | | | Insinkerator Evolution 5/8 HP (standard) | | |
| 152 | | | .75 HP Garbage Disposal | | |
| 153 | | Garbage Disposal | Air Switch | | |
| 154 | | | | | |
| 155 | 3600 | **Plumbing Features** | | | |
| 156 | | | Stainless Steel Sink | | |
| 157 | | | Quartz Sink | | |
| 158 | | | Cast Iron Sink | | |
| 159 | | | Single bowl, 50/50, 60/40 | | |
| 160 | | | Farm Sink | | |
| 161 | | Kitchen Sink | Stainless Steel Bar Sink | | |
| 162 | | | Luxart | | |
| 163 | | | Moen | | |
| 164 | | Kitchen Faucet | Kohler | | |
| 165 | | | Drop in Stainless Steel | | |
| 166 | | | Undermount Stainless Steel | | |
| 167 | | Utility | Faucet | | |
| 168 | | | Master Bath Commode - 1.6 Elongated | | |
| 169 | | | Master Bath Commode - 1.6 Elongated Comfort Height | | |

| 170 | | | Powder Commode - 1.6 Elongated | | |
|---|---|---|---|---|---|
| 171 | | | Powder Commode - 1.6 Elongated Comfort Height | | |
| 172 | | | Bath 1 Commode - 1.6 Elongated | | |
| 173 | | | Bath 1 Commode - 1.6 Elongated Comfort Height | | |
| 174 | | | Bath 2 Commode - 1.6 Elongated | | |
| 175 | | | Bath 2 Commode - 1.6 Elongated Comfort Height | | |
| 176 | | | Commode Color - WHITE | | |
| 177 | | Commodes | Commode Color - Biscuit | | |
| 178 | | | Furniture Piece | | |
| 179 | | | Custom cabinet with counter and UM Sink | | |
| 180 | | Powder Bath Sink | Pedestal Sink - 8" widespread Faucet | | |
| 181 | | | Luxart | | |
| 182 | | | Moen | | |
| 183 | | | Kohler | | |
| 184 | | Powder Bath Fixtures | Finish - Chrome, Satin Nickel, Oil Rubbed Bronze | | |
| 185 | | | Luxart | | |
| 186 | | | Moen | | |
| 187 | | | Kohler | | |
| 188 | | Master Bath Fixtures | Finish - Chrome, Satin Nickel, Oil Rubbed Bronze | | |
| 189 | | | Round Undermount | | |
| 190 | | | Square Undermount | | |
| 191 | | Master Bath Lavatory | Per Plan | | |
| 192 | | | Luxart | | |
| 193 | | | Moen | | |
| 194 | | | Kohler | | |
| 195 | | Bath 1 Fixtures | Finish - Chrome, Satin Nickel, Oil Rubbed Bronze | | |
| 196 | | | Round Undermount | | |
| 197 | | | Square Undermount | | |
| 198 | | Bath 1 Lavatory | Per Plan | | |
| 199 | | | Luxart | | |
| 200 | | | Moen | | |
| 201 | | | Kohler | | |
| 202 | | Bath 2 Fixtures | Finish - Chrome, Satin Nickel, Oil Rubbed Bronze | | |
| 203 | | | Round Undermount | | |
| 204 | | | Square Undermount | | |
| 205 | | Bath 2 Lavatory | Per Plan | | |
| 206 | | | 6' long oval - no jets | | |
| 207 | | | 6' long oval with jets | | |
| 208 | | Master Bath Tub | Per plan | | |
| 209 | | | Fiberglass Shower Pan | | |
| 210 | | | Solid Surface Shower Pan | | |
| 211 | | | Recessed Tile Mud Pan - UL Liner | | |
| 212 | | Shower Pans | Recessed Tile Mud Pan - Fiberglass (2nd Story - mandatory Fiberglass) | | |
| 213 | | | 6' Acrylic/Plastic Bath Tub | | |

| 214 | | Secondary Tubs | 6' Cast Iron Bath Tub | | |
|---|---|---|---|---|---|
| 215 | | | | | |
| 216 | 3700 | **Electric Base** | | | |
| 217 | | | Smoke Detectors | | |
| 218 | | | Carbon monoxide detector | | |
| 219 | | | Decora Rocker Switches | | |
| 220 | | | Rocker Switch Color - White or Biscuit | | |
| 221 | | | Garage Door Opener wiring | | |
| 222 | | | Jetted Tub Wiring | | |
| 223 | | | Dedicated Sprinkler Circuit | | |
| 224 | | | Dedicated Media Room Circuit | | |
| 225 | | | Control 4/Crestron/RTI/Lutron | | |
| 226 | | | 4 Fans Block and Wire - (Master bedroom, sitting area and x2 on Patio) | | |
| 227 | | | 3 Fans Block and Wire - (Family, Master and Gameroom) Block only at other locations | | |
| 228 | | Ceiling Fans - Prewire Only | Block and Wire Family, Retreat and all bedrooms | | |
| 229 | | | | | |
| 230 | 3800 | **HVAC** | | | |
| 231 | | | 14 SEER HVAC - Lennox or TRANE | | |
| 232 | | | 16 SEER HVAC - Lennox or TRANE (Variable Speed) | | |
| 233 | | | 19 SEER HVAC - Lennox or TRANE (Variable Speed) | | |
| 234 | | | 21 SEER HVAC - Lennox or TRANE (Variable Speed) | | |
| 235 | | | Geo Thermal | | |
| 236 | | | Heat Pump or Gas Furnace | | |
| 237 | | | Thermostat - Standard | | |
| 238 | | | Thermostat - NEST | | |
| 239 | | | Thermostat - IP over network (see structured wiring 3900) | | |
| 240 | | | 80% Efficient Gas Furnace - Normal Insulation | | |
| 241 | | | 90% Efficient Gas Furnace - Foam Insulation | | |
| 242 | | | Jump Ducts | | |
| 243 | | | Dedicated Returns | | |
| 244 | | | | | |
| 245 | 3900 | **Security** | | | |
| 246 | | | Prewire Only | | |
| 247 | | | All operable doors and windows monitored | | |
| 248 | | | Prewire & Trim 6 Zone System with 1 key pad | | |
| 249 | | | Prewire & Trim 6 Zone System with 2 key pads | | |
| 250 | | | Prewire for security cameras | | |
| 251 | | | | | |
| 252 | 3900 | **Structured Wiring A/V** | | | |
| 253 | | | 2x2 - 2 Cat 6 drops and 2 RG6 | | |
| 254 | | Standard | One room 5.1 surround sound prewire | | |
| 255 | | Additional Room | adds one additional multimedia | | |
| 256 | | Media Room | Adds one additional multimedia + 5.1 Surround Sound prewire | | |

| | | | | | |
|---|---|---|---|---|---|
| 257 | | | Projection Screen | | |
| 258 | | | Flat Screen | | |
| 259 | | | THX Certified Audio | | |
| 260 | | | Control 4, Crestron or RTI | | |
| 261 | | | Blinds | | |
| 262 | | | Lighting Control | | |
| 263 | | | HVAC | | |
| 264 | | Automation | Misc 1 - | | |
| 265 | | | Enterprise grade network | | |
| 266 | | Networking | Fiber cabling | | |
| 267 | | | | | |
| 268 | 4700 | **Insulation** | | | |
| 269 | | | Poly Seal (Standard) | | |
| 270 | | | Blown Cellulose | | |
| 271 | | | Foam Insulation | | |
| 272 | | | Open Cell | | |
| 273 | | | Closed Cell | | |
| 274 | | | Hybrid Foam - Walls and Ceiling Joists (attic not temperature controlled) | | |
| 275 | | | Sound Deadening (interior walls) | | |
| 276 | | House Wrap | Tyvek | | |
| 277 | | Exterior Wall | R-19 | | |
| 278 | | Sloped Ceiling | R-22 | | |
| 279 | | Flat Ceiling | R-38 | | |
| 280 | | Attic Wall | R-19 | | |
| 281 | | | | | |
| 282 | 5000 | **Drywall** | | | |
| 283 | | | Screw Sheetrock | | |
| 284 | | | Moisture Resistant Sheetrock | | |
| 285 | | | Sag resistant ceiling | | |
| 286 | | | Square Sheetrock Corners | | |
| 287 | | | Rounded Sheetrock Corners | | |
| 288 | | | Resilient Channel | | |
| 289 | | | Quietrock (recommeded for media room walls) | | |
| 290 | | | Orange Peel | | |
| 291 | | | Splatter Drag | | |
| 292 | | | Hand Trowel | | |
| 293 | | Finish | Slick Wall | | |
| 294 | | | | | |
| 295 | 4900 | **Paint** | | | |
| 296 | | | Walls and Ceilings Same Color | | |
| 297 | | | Walls and Ceilings different Color | | |
| 298 | | | Accent color in all art niches, groin vaults, media and pop up ceilings (1 color) | | |
| 299 | | | Sherwinn Williams Matte latex paint on walls and ceilings | | |
| 300 | | | Sherwinn Williams Satin enamel paint on trim | | |
| 301 | | | Sherwinn Williams Satin exterior latex paint on trim and siding | | |
| 302 | | | Sherwinn Williams Satin enamel paint on cabinets | | |
| 303 | | | Faux finish on cabinets or walls | | |
| 304 | | | Brand Preference - PPG, Benjamin Moore, Glidden | | |
| 305 | | | | | |
| 306 | 5350 | **Wall Tile - Baths/Kitchen** | | | |
| 307 | | | One Layer hardibacker | | |
| 308 | | All Showers | All 2nd floor or above must have fiberglass membrane | | |
| 309 | | | Level 1 Tile | | |
| 310 | | | Level 2 Tile | | |
| 311 | | Master bath - Wall Tile | Level 3 Tile | | |
| 312 | | | Level 1 Tile | | |
| 313 | | | Level 2 Tile | | |
| 314 | | Master bath - Tile Skirt | Level 3 Tile | | |
| 315 | | | Level 1 Tile | | |
| 316 | | | Level 2 Tile | | |
| 317 | | | Level 3 Tile | | |
| 318 | | Master Bath - Tub Deck | Granite Tub Deck | | |
| 319 | | | Fiberglass membrane | | |
| 320 | | | Level 1 Tile - 2x2 | | |
| 321 | | Master Bath - Shower Floor | Level 2 Tile - 2x2 | | |
| 322 | | | Fiberglass membrane | | |
| 323 | | | Level 1 Tile | | |
| 324 | | | Level 2 Tile | | |
| 325 | | Secondary Baths - Shower Surround | Level 3 Tile | | |
| 326 | | | Level 1 Tile | | |
| 327 | | | Level 2 Tile | | |
| 328 | | | Level 3 Tile | | |
| 329 | | | No Backsplash | | |
| 330 | | | Granite Backsplash - Full Height | | |
| 331 | | Kitchen Backsplash | Granite Backsplash - 4" | | |
| 332 | | | | | |
| 333 | 5100 | **Flooring** | | | |
| 334 | | | Level 1 | | |
| 335 | | | Level 2 | | |
| 336 | | | Level 3 | | |
| 337 | | | Level 4 | | |
| 338 | | Carpet | Level 5 | | |
| 339 | | | Level A - 3/8" Pad (5# rebound) | | |
| 340 | | | Level B - 1/2" Pad (6# rebound) | | |
| 341 | | Carpet Pad | Level A - 1/2" Pad (6# rebound) Stain Master | | |
| 342 | | | Level 1 | | |
| 343 | | | Level 2 | | |

| 344 | | | Level 3 | | |
|---|---|---|---|---|---|
| 345 | | | Level 4 | | |
| 346 | | Tile | Level 5 | | |
| 347 | | | 2 1/4" Nail down oak | | |
| 348 | | | 3" Nail Down Oak | | |
| 349 | | | 4" Nail Down Oak | | |
| 350 | | | No hand scrape | | |
| 351 | | | Hand scrape with the grain | | |
| 352 | | Wood - Nail Down | Hand scrape against the grain | | |
| 353 | | | Level 1 | | |
| 354 | | | Level 2 | | |
| 355 | | | Level 3 | | |
| 356 | | | Level 4 | | |
| 357 | | Wood - Engineered | Level 5 | | |
| 358 | | | Epoxy (2 part epoxy) | | |
| 359 | | | Rubber Flooring (Roll or Tile) | | |
| 360 | | Garage | Standard Concrete | | |
| 361 | | | | | |
| 362 | 5150 | **Interior Trim** | | | |
| 363 | | | Paint Grade | | |
| 364 | | Door Jambs | Stain Grade | | |
| 365 | | | 6'-8" - 2 Panel Foam Core | | |
| 366 | | | 6'-8" Solid Core Downstairs (Upstairs 6'8" foam core) | | |
| 367 | | | 8'-0" Solid Core Downstairs (Upstairs 6'8" foam core) | | |
| 368 | | | 8'-0" Solid Core Downstairs (Upstairs 6'8" solid core) | | |
| 369 | | | 8'-0" Solid Core Downstairs and Upstairs | | |
| 370 | | | Paint Grade - Masonite (Standard or Upgraded Bellagio) | | |
| 371 | | Interior Doors | Stain Grade - Smooth Alder | | |
| 372 | | | 1 piece 6" tall base | | |
| 373 | | | 2 piece 6" tall base | | |
| 374 | | | 1 piece 8" tall base | | |
| 375 | | | 2 piece 8" tall base | | |
| 376 | | | Stain Grade | | |
| 377 | | Base | Paint Grade | | |
| 378 | | | No crown | | |
| 379 | | | Single - MDF Bedroom and Baths | | |
| 380 | | | Single - #WM-45 MDF Entry, Dining, Formal Living, Study | | |
| 381 | | | Double - #8012 MDF w/ WM623 base (9" total) Entry, Dining, Formal Living, Study | | |
| 382 | | | Three Step Crown | | |
| 383 | | | Stain Grade | | |
| 384 | | Crown Mould | Paint Grade | | |
| 385 | | Chair Rail | CR-7 (2 1/2") @ dining | | |
| 386 | | | Sheetrock | | |
| 387 | | Plant Shelves | 3/4" MDF | | |
| 388 | | | MDF | | |
| 389 | | | MDF - Flat edge with M&M 144 screen mould on front of shelf | | |
| 390 | | | Wood Rods | | |
| 391 | | | Metal Rods | | |
| 392 | | | Seasonal rack - 3rd hanging space (10' tall ceilings mandatory) | | |
| 393 | | | Built onsite with MDF (Paint Grade) | | |
| 394 | | | Custom Design by Specialty Closet Design Company | | |
| 395 | | Closets | | | |
| 396 | | | Cedar Beams | | |
| 397 | | Beams | Faux Beams | | |
| 398 | | | | | |
| 399 | 5200 | **Stairs** | | | |
| 400 | | | Paint Grade | | |
| 401 | | | Metal Twist Balusters | | |
| 402 | | Balusters | Decorative Panels | | |
| 403 | | | Stain Grade | | |
| 404 | | Newels | Metal | | |
| 405 | | | Stain Grade | | |
| 406 | | | Metal | | |
| 407 | | | Solid Surface | | |
| 408 | | Handrail | Hand Rail inset in wall | | |
| 409 | | | 1x12 MDF Paint Grade | | |
| 410 | | Stair Skirt | 1x12 Stain Grade Oak | | |
| 411 | | | 1x8 MDF | | |
| 412 | | Tread Caps | Stained Grade | | |
| 413 | | | None - Carpet to floor | | |
| 414 | | | Full Starter Step - Oak | | |
| 415 | | | All Treads Oak | | |
| 416 | | | Solid Surface Treads | | |
| 417 | | Treads | Metal Stair | | |
| 418 | | | Paint | | |
| 419 | | | Stain | | |
| 420 | | Risers | Tile | | |
| 421 | | | MDF Primed | | |
| 422 | | | Solid Surface | | |
| 423 | | Window Stool | Natural Stone | | |
| 424 | | Box Window Seat | MDF Primed | | |
| 425 | | | Shoe Mould at Tile & Wood Areas | | |
| 426 | | Shoe Mold | No Shoe Mould | | |
| 427 | | | | | |
| 428 | 5150/5350 | **Fireplace Surround** | | | |
| 429 | | | No Legs - Paint Grade - Tile Surround (Level 1) | | |
| 430 | | | Legs - Paint Grade - Tile Surround (Level 1) | | |

| | | | | | |
|---|---|---|---|---|---|
| 431 | | | Legs - Stain Grade - Tile Surround (Level 2) | | |
| 432 | | Mantel - Built on Site | Legs - Paint Grade - Tile Surround (Level 2) | | |
| 433 | | | Natural Stone Surround - 60" tall (match column | | |
| 434 | | | Limestone Surround | | |
| 435 | | | Granite/Marble Surround | | |
| 436 | | Natural Stone Mantel | Overmantle | | |
| 437 | | | Cedar | | |
| 438 | | | Cast Stone Surround | | |
| 439 | | Outdoor Mantel | Limestone Surround | | |
| 440 | | | Wood attic Access | | |
| 441 | | | Metal Attic access | | |
| 442 | | Attic Access | Pull down rod (ceilings 10' and higher) | | |
| 443 | | | | | |
| 444 | 5270 | **Hardware** | | | |
| 445 | | | Luxart - Chrome | | |
| 446 | | | Luxart - Satin Nickel | | |
| 447 | | | Luxart - Oil Rubbed Bronze | | |
| 448 | | | Moen - Chrome | | |
| 449 | | | Moen - Satin Nickel | | |
| 450 | | | Moen - Oil Rubbed Bronze | | |
| 451 | | Bathrooms | Other brand | | |
| 452 | | | Master - 1 towel ring per sink, 1 paper holder, 1 towel bar 24" | | |
| 453 | | | Powder - 1 towel ring per sink, 1 paper holder | | |
| 454 | | | Secondary - 1 towel ring per sink, 1 paper holder, 1 towel bar 24" | | |
| 455 | | Bath Hardware | Other brand | | |
| 456 | | | Granduer - Round knobs - Satin Nickel | | |
| 457 | | | Granduer - Round knobs - Oil Rubbed Bronze | | |
| 458 | | | Granduer - Lever knobs - Satin Nickel | | |
| 459 | | | Granduer - Lever knobs - Oil Rubbed Bronze | | |
| 460 | | Interior Door Hardware | Other Brand | | |
| 461 | | Exterior Door Hardware - Front | Keyset and Deadbolt | | |
| 462 | | | Garage to House - Keyset and Deadbolt | | |
| 463 | | Exterior Door Hardware - Other/Rear | Other Exterior Doors - Keyset and Deadbolt | | |
| 464 | | | Satin Nickel | | |
| 465 | | Heavy Duty Door Stops | Oil Rubbed Bronze | | |
| 466 | | | | | |
| 467 | 4100/5350 | **Address Plaque** | | | |
| 468 | | | Metal | | |
| 469 | | | Cast Stone | | |
| 470 | | | | | |
| 471 | 5400 | **Cabinets** | | | |
| 472 | | | Prefinished | | |
| 473 | | | Paint Grade | | |
| 474 | | | Stain Grade Knotty Alder | | |

| | | | | | |
|---|---|---|---|---|---|
| 475 | | | Stain Grade Other | | |
| 476 | | | Maple | | |
| 477 | | | 30" Upper Cabinets | | |
| 478 | | | 42" Upper Cabinets | | |
| 479 | | | Euro-style Doors (frameless) | | |
| 480 | | | Inset Doors/Drawers (Doors and drawers line up with face frame) | | |
| 481 | | | Full Overlay Doors | | |
| 482 | | Kitchen | Glass Doors | | |
| 483 | | Butler Pantry | Same Species/Style as Kitchen | | |
| 484 | | Family Room Built in | Same Species/Style as Kitchen | | |
| 485 | | | Furniture Piece | | |
| 486 | | | Paint Grade | | |
| 487 | | | Stain Grade | | |
| 488 | | | 35" tall Cabinets | | |
| 489 | | | 30" tall Cabinets | | |
| 490 | | Master Bath | Headknocker - Cabinet above commode | | |
| 491 | | | Furniture Piece | | |
| 492 | | | Paint Grade | | |
| 493 | | | Stain Grade | | |
| 494 | | | 35" tall Cabinets | | |
| 495 | | | 30" tall Cabinets | | |
| 496 | | Secondary Baths | Headknocker - Cabinet above commode | | |
| 497 | | | Furniture Piece | | |
| 498 | | | Paint Grade | | |
| 499 | | | Stain Grade | | |
| 500 | | | 35" tall Cabinets | | |
| 501 | | | 30" tall Cabinets | | |
| 502 | | Powder Bath | No cabinet - pedestal | | |
| 503 | | Bank of Drawers | Locations and Quantity | | |
| 504 | | Built-In Desk | Same Species/Style as Kitchen | | |
| 505 | | TV Niche | Same Species/Style as Kitchen | | |
| 506 | | | No Cabinets - Fixed Shelf and Rod per plan | | |
| 507 | | | One 36x30 Cabinet with rod - Species same as kitchen | | |
| 508 | | Utility Room | Per plan | | |
| 509 | | | Storage Cabinets (enclosed) | | |
| 510 | | Garage | Open Shelves | | |
| 511 | | | | | |
| 512 | | | | | |
| 513 | 5300 | **Countertops** | | | |
| 514 | | | Granite - Level 1 | | |
| 515 | | | Granite - Level 2 | | |
| 516 | | | Granite - Level 3 | | |
| 517 | | | Granite - Level 4 | | |
| 518 | | | Granite - Level 5 | | |

| | | | | | |
|---|---|---|---|---|---|
| 519 | | | Quartz - Level 1 | | |
| 520 | | | Quartz - Level 2 | | |
| 521 | | | Quartz - Level 3 | | |
| 522 | | | Quartz - Level 4 | | |
| 523 | | Kitchen | Quartz - Level 5 | | |
| 524 | | Butler's Pantry | Match Kitchen Material/Color/Edge | | |
| 525 | | | Granite - Level 1 | | |
| 526 | | | Granite - Level 2 | | |
| 527 | | | Granite - Level 3 | | |
| 528 | | | Granite - Level 4 | | |
| 529 | | | Granite - Level 5 | | |
| 530 | | | Quartz - Level 1 | | |
| 531 | | | Quartz - Level 2 | | |
| 532 | | | Quartz - Level 3 | | |
| 533 | | | Quartz - Level 4 | | |
| 534 | | Master Bath | Quartz - Level 5 | | |
| 535 | | | Granite - Level 1 | | |
| 536 | | | Granite - Level 2 | | |
| 537 | | | Quartz - Level 1 | | |
| 538 | | Utility | Quartz - Level 2 | | |
| 539 | | | Granite - Level 1 | | |
| 540 | | | Granite - Level 2 | | |
| 541 | | | Granite - Level 3 | | |
| 542 | | | Granite - Level 4 | | |
| 543 | | | Quartz - Level 1 | | |
| 544 | | | Quartz - Level 2 | | |
| 545 | | | Quartz - Level 3 | | |
| 546 | | Secondary Baths | Quartz - Level 4 | | |
| 547 | | | Wood Countertops | | |
| 548 | | | Natural Stone | | |
| 549 | | Cabinet Built-In Tops | Locations | | |
| 550 | | | | | |
| 551 | 4100 | **Brick** | | | |
| 552 | | | Not Applicable | | |
| 553 | | | 100% Brick Whole Home | | |
| 554 | | | 80% Brick - Siding in back | | |
| 555 | | | Brick entire first floor, 3 sides second floor | | |
| 556 | | | Brick Mailbox | | |
| 557 | | | Brick Color? | | |
| 558 | | | Modular, Queen or King Size | | |
| 559 | | | Brick Color? | | |
| 560 | | | Per plan | | |
| 561 | | | Grey Mortar | | |
| 562 | | | Buff Mortar (If Stone, mortar will be buff or white) | | |

| | | | | | |
|---|---|---|---|---|---|
| 563 | | Mortar | White Mortar (If Stone, mortar will be buff or white) | | |
| 564 | | Lintels | Pre-primed Steel | | |
| 565 | | | | | |
| 566 | 4100 | **Natural Stone** | | | |
| 567 | | | Not Applicable | | |
| 568 | | | Natural or Synthetic Stone | | |
| 569 | | | Water Table | | |
| 570 | | | Front Entry | | |
| 571 | | | Detail Per Plan | | |
| 572 | | | Random Pattern | | |
| 573 | | | Chiseled Pattern | | |
| 574 | | | | | |
| 575 | 5050 | **Stucco** | | | |
| 576 | | | 3 Coat True Stucco Application | | |
| 577 | | | Integral Color (Color mixed into stucco on last coat) | | |
| 578 | | | Elastro-merick crack suppressant | | |
| 579 | | | | | |
| 580 | 4100 | **Cast Stone/Limestone** | | | |
| 581 | | | Exterior Window Sills | | |
| 582 | | | Exterior Window Surrounds | | |
| 583 | | | Water Table | | |
| 584 | | | Entry Suround | | |
| 585 | | | Juliet Baclony Surround | | |
| 586 | | | | | |
| 587 | 4200 | **Fireplace** | | | |
| 588 | | | Wood Burning Fireplace | | |
| 589 | | | Gas Fireplace | | |
| 590 | | | Gas Fireplace - B Vent | | |
| 591 | | | Auto Igniter | | |
| 592 | | | 36" Metal Box | | |
| 593 | | | 42" Metal Box | | |
| 594 | | | 36" Isokern | | |
| 595 | | | 42" Isokern | | |
| 596 | | | Isokern Height Extension | | |
| 597 | | | | | |
| 598 | 5500 | **Appliances** | | | |
| 599 | | | GE Café | | |
| 600 | | | Thermador | | |
| 601 | | | Viking | | |
| 602 | | | Wolf/SubZero | | |
| 603 | | Wine Fridge | Per Plan | | |
| 604 | | Outdoor Living | Per Plan | | |
| 605 | | | | | |
| 606 | 3700 | **Lighting** | | | |
| 607 | | | Customer Color Selections | | |

| 608 | | | Sconces - | | |
|---|---|---|---|---|---|
| 609 | | | Chandaliers | | |
| 610 | | | Vanity - | | |
| 611 | | Interior/Exterior | Other - | | |
| 612 | | | Can light 6" | | |
| 613 | | | Can light other | | |
| 614 | | | Flourescent in garage | | |
| 615 | | | Can lights in Garage | | |
| 616 | | | Closets on Jamb switch | | |
| 617 | | | Flourescent in closets | | |
| 618 | | Cans/Flourescent/Keyless | Can lights in closet | | |
| 619 | | | CFL - Compact Flourescents | | |
| 620 | | Light Bulbs | LED - Light Emitting Diodes | | |
| 621 | | | | | |
| 622 | | | | | |
| 623 | 5900 | **Shower Doors** | | | |
| 624 | | | Framed Enclosure | | |
| 625 | | | Frameless Enclosure - 3/8" Glass | | |
| 626 | | | Satin Nickle Harware | | |
| 627 | | Master Bath | Oil Rubbed Bronze Hardware | | |
| 628 | | | Rod Only | | |
| 629 | | | Framed Enclosure | | |
| 630 | | | Frameless Enclosure - 3/8" Glass | | |
| 631 | | | Satin Nickle Harware | | |
| 632 | | Secondary Baths | Oil Rubbed Bronze Hardware | | |
| 633 | | | | | |
| 634 | 5950 | **Mirrors/Glass** | | | |
| 635 | | | 42" wide Beveled | | |
| 636 | | | Full length - Belveled | | |
| 637 | | Master Bath | Frame Mirror | | |
| 638 | | | 42" wide Beveled | | |
| 639 | | | Full length - Belveled | | |
| 640 | | Secondary Baths | Frame Mirror | | |
| 641 | | | Octagon Beveled Mirror | | |
| 642 | | Powder | 24" x 36" Framed Mirror | | |
| 643 | | Other Rooms | Mirrored Walls | | |
| 644 | | | Glass Shelves | | |
| 645 | | | Glass Inserts | | |
| 646 | | Cabinets | Mirror Inserts | | |
| 647 | | | | | |
| 648 | | | | | |
| 649 | 3700 | **Ceiling Fans** | | | |
| 650 | | | Family Room | | |
| 651 | | | Master Bedroom | | |
| 652 | | | Gameroom | | |
| 653 | | | Media Room | | |
| 654 | | | Secondary Bedrooms | | |
| 655 | | | Exterior - Patio | | |
| 656 | | | | | |
| 657 | 6300 | **Fence** | | | |
| 658 | | | 6' Spruce Fence - 4x4 wood posts to middle or back corner of house | | |
| 659 | | | 6' Cedar Fence - 4x4 wood posts to middle or back corner of house | | |
| 660 | | | 6' Cedar Fence - Metal posts to middle or back corner of house | | |
| 661 | | | 8' Cedar Fence - Metal posts to middle or back corner of house | | |
| 662 | | | Board on Board | | |
| 663 | | | Top cap | | |
| 664 | | | Rot board | | |
| 665 | | | Wrought Iron Fence | | |
| 666 | | | 1 Gate | | |
| 667 | | | 2 Gates | | |
| 668 | | | Bring fence forward to front of house | | |
| 669 | | | | | |
| 670 | 3510 | **Gutters** | | | |
| 671 | | | Partial (Front and Rear Porch) | | |
| 672 | | | Seamless Metal (color matched to eves) or Precious Metal (Copper) | | |
| 673 | | | Full gutters | | |
| 674 | | | Leaf Guards | | |
| 675 | | | Bird's Nest | | |
| 676 | | | Square downspouts | | |
| 677 | | | Round downspouts | | |
| 678 | | | | | |
| 679 | 4500 | **Garage Door** | | | |
| 680 | | | Metal Garage Door - No Insulation | | |
| 681 | | | Metal Garage Door with Insulation | | |
| 682 | | | Metal Garage Door with wood overlay | | |
| 683 | | | Cedar Garage Door | | |
| 684 | | | Glass Garage Door | | |
| 685 | | | 8' garage doors | | |
| 686 | | | 9' garage doors | | |
| 687 | | | Single 16' garage door | | |
| 688 | | | Single 18' garage door | | |
| 689 | | | Single 16' garage door and single 8' garage door (3 car garage) | | |
| 690 | | | 1/2 hp garage door opener | | |
| 691 | | | 1/3 hp garage door opener | | |
| 692 | | | Standard Ceiling Mount Garage door Opener | | |
| 693 | | | Wall Mount/Side Mount/Jack shaft Mount Opener | | |
| 694 | | | | | |
| 695 | 6100 | **Trees** | | | |

| | | | | | |
|---|---|---|---|---|---|
| 696 | | | # of trees - | | |
| 697 | | | Pruning or Removal? | | |
| 698 | | | Maintenance Program? | | |
| 699 | | | Root Barrier Needed | | |
| 700 | | | Temporary Fencing around trees during construction? | | |
| 701 | | | Budget | | |
| 702 | | | | | |
| 703 | 6180 | **Automatic Lawn** | | | |
| 704 | | | # of zones | | |
| 705 | | | Full with Rain Freeze Sensor | | |
| 706 | | | Control Panel in Garage | | |
| 707 | | | | | |
| 708 | 6105 | **Sod** | | | |
| 709 | | | Full Sod | | |
| 710 | | | Bermuda | | |
| 711 | | | St Augustine | | |
| 712 | | | Zoysia | | |
| 713 | | | Other | | |
| 714 | | | | | |
| 715 | 6106 | **Shrubs** | | | |
| 716 | | | Budget - | | |
| 717 | | | | | |

# Invoice:

Ref Name/No.: ABC Project

Invoice Date: 07/29/2021

**2[g] Habitats**
4400 TX-121
Suite 300
Lewisville, Texas 75056
Phone: (214) 850-8313
Hello@2gHabitats.com

| Date: | Name: | Cost: |
|---|---|---|
| 07/29/2021 | 5012 – Sheetrock Materials<br>*Estimated Budget - $10,000* | $5,000.00 |
| 07/29/2021 | 5013 – Drywall Labor<br>*Estimated Budget - $7500* | $2,000.00 |
| 07/29/2021 | 3110 – Frame Lumber<br>*Estimated Budget - $15,000* | $10,000.00 |
| 07/29/2021 | 3151 - Frame Labor<br>*Estimated Budget - $12,000* | $5,000.00 |
| 07/29/2021 | 1090 – Misc. Permits/Fees<br>*Asbestos inspection for City of Dallas and TDLR Registration* | $1,000.00 |

Total: $ 23,000.00

## First Team Meeting:

Proper communication between the builder and homeowner makes the 2[g] Habitats' building experience enjoyable and effective. In our 1st team meeting, we will be setting the proper expectations to minimize unexpected issues that may occur during the building and planning phase of construction.

| INITIALS | ITEM |
|---|---|
| | The purpose and details of the 1st team meeting, Pre-Drywall meeting and Homeowner Introduction have been explained to me. |
| | I understand and agree to relay all communications regarding the construction of my home via email, or verbally at our construction meetings. |
| | I understand that NO extra work (that deviates from original plan) will be performed without an approved change order. |
| | I understand that I am not allowed to do any work, or independently contract work, to be done on my home prior to closing. |
| | I understand that there may not be observable work evident for periods of time during the construction process. |
| | The appropriate slope of my yard and driveway has been reviewed and I understand that 2[g] Habitats will not install retaining walls unless it exceeds the required slope criteria. |
| | I understand that there may be repair items. The repair of these items may be postponed due to future incidents of a similar nature arising.<br>**Example:**<br>*Exterior items may be postponed until the final grading work on your yard is completed *Drywall repairs will be completed after the electrical trim is completed *Window repairs will be postponed until brick and stucco work is completed |
| | I understand that when a natural material is used, there can be variations in color and texture, and that this is an unavoidable characteristic.<br>**Example:**<br>*Brick and Stone may vary slightly in color, texture, and/or shape, and there can be cracking *The finish on wood floors and cabinets can look inconsistent *When staining wood it may take the stain differently in various areas. Also, stains may look different depending on the wood species *Granite, Travertine or Marble will always have movement and color variations |
| | I understand that 2[g] Habitats considers any item that cannot be pointed out from an arm's length, as too minute to require repairs. This is important to remember |

| | during the "New Home Orientation". |
|---|---|
| | I understand that hairline cracks are an inherent nature of concrete foundations, sidewalks, patios, and driveways. However, 2[g] Habitats will take precautionary measures to minimize cracking. |
| | I understand that 2[g] Habitats does not commit to placing certain items in exact locations.<br>**Example:**<br>*AC vents, thermostats, return air vents, condensing units, electric gas, water meters, exterior water spigots, as well as interior and exterior electric plugs. *If you are wanting these items to be located in certain areas, please make that request to your builder and they will try to accommodate it if possible. |
| | I understand that if there are native trees on my lot, 2[g] Habitats will not be responsible for their health. 2[g] Habitats will be waived of any and all liabilities involving native trees after closing. |

| **Buyer** | |
|---|---|
| **Address** | |
| **Date** | |

| Signatures: |
|---|
| By signing below, I acknowledge that I have a thorough understanding of the expectations between 2[g] Habitats and the homeowner as outlined in this document. |

________________________________
Homeowner

________________________________
Date

________________________________
Builder

________________________________
Date

## Pre-Drywall Meeting:

Proper communication between the builder and homeowner makes the 2[g] Habitats building experience enjoyable and effective. In our pre-drywall meeting, we will be discussing items that have been completed thus far in your home. Some of the items include electrical, low voltage, and plumbing. It is important that the placement of these items are thoroughly understood and reviewed. If you have any questions, or would like to have an item moved, please voice your concerns now. Once sheetrock is in place, these items cannot be moved without incurring significant costs. This is an important step in the collaboration process, as we strive to deliver the completed home to you in a timely manner.

| INITIALS | ITEM |
|---|---|
| | Electrical plug and switch locations |
| | Can and mini can light locations |
| | Ceiling fan locations |
| | Interior light fixture locations |
| | Exterior light locations |
| | Under counter and over counter light locations |
| | Vanity light locations |
| | Electric meter locations |

| | |
|---|---|
| | Cable outlet locations |
| | Phone jack locations |
| | Other A/V and data outlet locations |
| | Speaker pre-wire locations |
| | Security keypad locations |

| | |
|---|---|
| | HVAC thermostat locations |
| | HVAC condenser locations |

| | |
|---|---|
| | Gas lamp locations (if applicable) |
| | Gas stub out locations (for BBQ or other locations) |
| | Gas meter locations |

| | |
|---|---|
| | Plumbing stub out locations (hose bibs, etc.) |

| | |
|---|---|
| | Gas lamp locations (if applicable) |
| | Gas stub out locations (for BBQ or other locations) |
| | Gas meter locations |

| | |
|---|---|
| | Fence locations including gates |

| **Buyer** | |
|---|---|
| **Address** | |
| **Date** | |

| Signatures: |
|---|
| By signing below, I acknowledge that I have a thorough understanding of the expectations between 2[g] Habitats and the homeowner as outlined in this document. |

________________________________________

Homeowner

________________________________________

Date

________________________________________

Builder

________________________________________

Date

# Homeowner Introduction Meeting:

Exterior Items

| | Topic | Details | Notes |
|---|---|---|---|
| | Water Meter | Shuts off water to entire home. | |
| | Concrete | Hairline cracks are normal. Discuss purpose of expansion and control joints. | |
| | Utility Lines | If underground settling of soil is covered for 30 days. | |
| | Drainage | Discuss importance of proper drainage. Swales may remain wet for up to 48 hours after rains stops. | |
| | Landscape | Review care and maintenance required. (Native trees not warrantable.) | |
| | Plumbing Cleanouts | Review main and individual clean-outs. | |
| | Water Cut-off | Shuts water off to the home. Leaves landscape sprinklers and fire sprinklers (if applicable) operable. | |
| | Sprinkler System | Review operation of double check valves, and control panel. Review freeze/rain sensor. | |
| | Secondary A/C Drain | Dripping indicates a clogged primary drain. | |
| | Weep Holes | Allow moisture to escape (brick) | |
| | Expansion Joints | In Stucco and brick – allow for expansion and contraction. | |
| | Roof Ventilation | Review purpose of soffit and roof vents. | |
| | A/C Disconnect | Discuss purpose at condenser. | |

Exterior Items Continued

| | Topic | Details | Notes |
|---|---|---|---|
| | Circuit Breaker Box | Review tripped breakers, labeling and main cut-off. | |
| | Fire Sprinkler System (if applicable) | Mani shutoff should always stay on. Review suggested annual testing/maintenance. | |

## Interior Items

| | Topic | Details | Notes |
|---|---|---|---|
| | Paint | Understand use of paint touch- up kit. | |
| | Drywall | Review maintenance of settling cracks with latex caulking. | |
| | Countertop Maintenance | Granite should be sealed yearly. Do not cut or put hot pots directly on surface. | |
| | Faucets and Commodes | Understand cleaning of aerators and operation of cut- offs. | |
| | Appliances | Review operation, maintenance, and warranty information. | |
| | Garbage Disposal | Understand jamming and location of reset button. | |
| | Switched Outlets | Review locations – outlets are placed upside down. | |
| | GFCI / AFCI | Understand operation and locations. | |
| | Plumbing Stoppage | Construction related stoppage is covered. | |

## Interior Items Continued

| | Topic | Details | Notes |
|---|---|---|---|
| | Tile | Review maintenance of grout cracking with tile caulking or regrouting. | |
| | Carpet | Regular vacuuming and cleaning will prolong its life. | |
| | Fireplace | Understand operation of screens, damper, and log lighter. Direct vent fireplaces – be careful near exterior vent. | |
| | Doors | Some adjustments may be necessary due to changing weather conditions. | |
| | Doorknobs | Occasional tightening may be necessary. | |
| | Smoke/CO Detectors | Understand operation. Change battery at least once per year – 9v battery. | |
| | Jetted Tubs | Water level should be 2" above jets before use. | |
| | HVAC Thermostat | Review and understand operation. | |
| | HVAC Filters | Discuss location and understand that changing filters regularly improves performance. | |
| | Furnace Switch | Terminates power to HVAC system. | |
| | Water Heaters | Understand purpose of T&P valves and annual draining. | |
| | Utilities | Remember to turn on utilities | |
| | Freezing Pipes | Understand cold weather preventative measures | |

## Warranty Coverage

| | Topic | Details |
|---|---|---|
| | 1 Year Coverage | Defects in materials and workmanship, excluding cosmetic items. |
| | 2 Year Coverage | Portions of the major mechanicals (heating and air conditioning), major electrical and major plumbing systems (not including electrical and plumbing fixtures such and faucets, shower heads and chandeliers). |
| | 10 Year Coverage | Major structural – foundation and load bearing frame |

Notes:

I have reviewed each of these with a 2[g] Habitats representative.

Customer Date

Builder Date

www.ingramcontent.com/pod-product-compliance
Lightning Source LLC
LaVergne TN
LVHW080557160826
845677LV00010B/1889

* 9 7 9 8 8 1 5 2 2 5 7 4 9 *